Dog-grr-el

Books by Nancy L. Reed

Words Left Behind: tales from a life gladly lived

A Short Story Olio

Dog-grr-el

canine cadence, hound haiku, puppy poetry

For Dog Lovers of All Ages

Nancy L. Reed

WOODEN PANTS PUBLISHING

Copyright© 2015 by Nancy L. Reed

All rights reserved.
This book or any portion thereof may not be reproduced or used in any manner whatsoever without the express written permission of the publisher.

978-0-692-54454-9
0692544542

Cover Art
Jennifer Schafer

Cover Canine
Libby Savannah Hennessee

Illustrations
Janice Glenn
Chris Nugent
Jennifer Schafer

Scores
Louise Meiman
Jasmine Schafer
Jennifer Schafer

First Printing 2015
Printed in the United States of America

Sign up for the Wooden Pants Publishing newsletter at www.woodenpantspub.com for the latest news about authors and publications.

DEDICATION

These poems and songs celebrate our loving companions who live life to the fullest

Satin, Bismarck, Moose, Belle Bête, Lily, Libby, Aislinn, Millie

All my canine friends – met and still to meet

ACKNOWLEDGEMENTS

Many thanks to the folks who helped make this a fun and beneficial project.

... Janice Glenn – for constructing Grr-ly and giving her personality.

... Chris Nugent – for being Grr-ly's favorite photographer.

... Jennifer Schafer – for her cover design and illustrations of Grr-ly.

... Louise Meiman – for getting the ball rolling on scoring the music.

... Jasmine Schafer – for her skill and patience in finalizing the musical scores.

CONTENTS

Canine Coat of Arms...1
Domain 1
Friend 1
Mornings 2
Flamenco 2
Dreams 2
A.Z.'s Song 3
Sacred Circles 4
Welcome 4
The Howllelujah Chorus 5
Story 5
Protect 5
Opposites 6
Walkies 6
Variations 6
Tribute to a Fire Hydrant 7
Bath 7
Swim 7
Cadence 8
Rescued Pooch 10
Resolution 12
Together 12
Play 12
P. P. Kadiddlehopper 13
Baton 13
Scraps 13
ready, set, go 14
Awaken 14
Thrills 14
Lilly's Song 15
Troglodog 16
Antediluvian 16
Smoglodog 16
Today 16
So Long For Now 17
Aging 17
Parting 17

Canine Coat of Arms

Crossed paws on field of grass,
Burly laddie, bonny lass,
A regal form 'gainst sky of blue
Proclaims the motto, "Always True."

Domain
Canine grass estate
Trees and bushes scrutinized
All accounted for

Friend
Sweet loving creature
Blind trusting obedience
Infinite giving

Mornings

The night is done,
The day's begun,
You want to run,
To go, go, go.

Out of bed,
Our walk's ahead,
You must be fed,
To help you grow.

I'm a mess,
I need to dress,
And I confess
I'm very slow.

I try to hurry
While you worry,
And you scurry
To and fro.

You are great,
You hesitate,
And always wait
When I say "Whoa!"

We're out the door
To smells galore
And to explore
In morning's glow.

Flamenco
Clickety-click-click
Multiplied a hundred fold
Dancing nails on floor

Dreams
Deadly still no breath
Jerk whimpering feet scuffling
High-speed rabbit chase

A.Z.'s Song

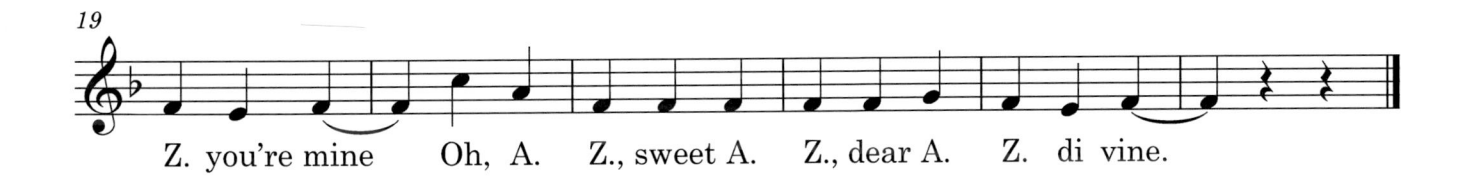

Oh, A. Z. Oh, A. Z. Oh, A. Z. you're cra zy You're fun-
ny, you're sun ny, you're my lit tle ho ney You're beau ti ful, du ti ful, some
times you're poo ti ful___ Oh, A. Z. Oh, A. Z. Oh, A.
Z. you're mine Oh, A. Z., sweet A. Z., dear A. Z. di vine.

Sacred Circles

Round and round and round you go
Some circles quick, some circles slow

    One … Mad dash clockwise
    Two … Circle car with purpose
    Three … Blessing complete, get in

Round and round and round you run
Some circles serious, some circles fun

    Three … Whirling dervish tight turn
    Two … Slightly slower, nose to tail
    One … Flop in bed, contented sigh

Round and round and round you speed
Sometimes the circles result from need

    One … Counter clockwise, concentrate
    Two … Seal the egress from the tree
    Three … Squirrel is trapped, can't come down

Round and round and round you spin
Circling out and circling in

    One … From door to me
    Two … Tacking tighter as I near
    Three … No time left, visitor to greet

Welcome

    Bright expectant face
    Quivering with greetings warm
    Well and truly home

The Howllelujah Chorus

The world is silent, deadly still,
Dawn's glimmer not yet born.
There is no whisper, no whimper.
All lie comatose beneath the black shroud of stars.

From far away a mechanical screech
Begins its rampage across the land,
Rising and falling from agony to relief,
Crashing its numbing message upon all creatures.

Those it reaches first begin the song,
Canine heads throw back in preparation,
Sleep-raspy throats vocalize a shrill serenade
Which moves inexorably in pulsating waves.

Alto, soprano, tenor, bass
Compose an extemporaneous score.
Creature voices, wild and domestic
Blend together in harmonious cacophony.

As the distressful noise passes,
Voices join in, then disengage
Until silence overcomes the chorus,
And the voices are again as still as death.

Bodies wearied by the painful joy
Return to slumber and to mindless dreams,
The memory of the symphony
Once more dormant in the morass of instinct.

Story
    Tell a tale of tail
    Wave and wag wonderingly
    Speak hairy volumes

Protect
    Lightning speed dashing
    Solid wood fence on alley
    Invisible foe

Opposites

My Honey, my Bun,
My Honey, my Bun,
I like to walk, you like to run,
But we can still have bundles of fun,
Honey Bun.

My Lovey, my Dove,
My Lovey, my Dove,
You tend to pull, and I tend to shove,
But we work together, a hand and a glove,
Lovey Dove.

My Darling, my Dear,
My Darling, my Dear,
You are there, and I am here.
Before you know it, we'll be quite near,
Darling Dear.

My Sweetie, my Pie,
My Sweetie, my Pie,
Some days are low and others are high.
We'll dream on the ground and reach for the sky,
Sweetie Pie.

My Dearie, my Heart,
My Dearie, my Heart,
Often together, sometimes apart.
Either way, we're still heart to heart,
Dearie Heart.

My Jumping, My Bean,
My Jumping, My Bean,
I may be fat, but you're always lean.
You are the cutest dog I've ever seen,
Jumping Bean.

Walkies
Leash at the ready
Anticipation abounds
Outside go go go

Variations
Sweet garners salty
Quiet gives way to raucous
Playing to respite

Tribute to a Fire Hydrant

I salute you, Proud Sentinel,
Keeper of the water pure.
Your iron stance
And steel resolve
Provide a lift
To leg and spirit.

Bath
    Cold wet porcelain
    Drooping tail streaming water
    Sad and soulful eyes

Swim
    Sparkling cold river
    Warm kiddy pool in back yard
    Splashing wet great fun

Cadence
A Marching Chant

I have a dog, her name is Dove.
She gives me lots of puppy love.
She likes to play and take a walk.
She has her special way to talk.

Chorus
Sound off ... Arf! Arf!
Sound off ... Woof! Woof!
Sound off ... Arf! Arf! Woof! Woof! Yip! Yip!

She picked up ticks. She picked up fleas.
A buggy dog just doesn't please.
I bombed the car, I bombed the house.
I killed off every single louse.

Chorus
Sound off ... Arf! Arf!
Sound off ... Woof! Woof!
Sound off ... Arf! Arf! Woof! Woof! Yip! Yip!

She grew up sweet. She grew up strong.
Her ears are short. Her tail is long.
Her coat is golden, silky fine.
I'm glad I'm hers, and she is mine.

Chorus
Sound off ... Arf! Arf!
Sound off ... Woof! Woof!
Sound off ... Arf! Arf! Woof! Woof! Yip! Yip!

Dove has some toys of softest fleece.
She never rips them with her teeth.
She plays with them and guards them too.
They're members of her private zoo.

Chorus
Sound off ... Arf! Arf!
Sound off ... Woof! Woof!
Sound off ... Arf! Arf! Woof! Woof! Yip! Yip!

She loves her toys, knows each by name,
And likes to play the choosing game.
I ask for Bear or Lady B,
She brings the right one back to me.

Chorus
Sound off ... Arf! Arf!
Sound off ... Woof! Woof!
Sound off ... Arf! Arf! Woof! Woof! Yip! Yip!

Dove likes to walk around the park.
She says Hello with wag and bark.
She sniffs the scents on trees and grass,
And every bench and bush we pass.

Chorus
Sound off ... Arf! Arf!
Sound off ... Woof! Woof!
Sound off ... Arf! Arf! Woof! Woof! Yip! Yip!

She has a friend, its name is Squirrel.
We don't know whether boy or girl.
They run and chatter, bark and whine.
They play in rain and bright sunshine.

Chorus
Sound off ... Arf! Arf!
Sound off ... Woof! Woof!
Sound off ... Arf! Arf! Woof! Woof! Yip! Yip!

I have a dog. Her name is Dove.
She gives me wags and licks and love.
She's more than just a pet, you see.
She's comfort, warmth, a friend to me.

Chorus
Sound off ... Arf! Arf!
Sound off ... Woof! Woof!
Sound off ... Arf! Arf! Woof! Woof! Yip! Yip!

Rescued Pooch

Li ly Pe tu nia Rasp ber ee, I'm glad you came to live with me, I promise your life will ne ver be the way it was be fore. Li ly Pe tu nia Rasp ber ray, We'll have fun both night and day, We'll cud dle and laugh and run and play, And joy will be our core. Li ly Pe tu nia Rasp ber roo, You like me, and I like you, Our friendship will be strong and true, From now to evermore Lily Petunia Raspbereye, We may laugh, and we may cry, But for all the lows we'll have more highs, remember *je t'adore*. Lily Petunia Raspberry This is the end of your song you see.

Resolution

I yell until I'm hoarse,
Throw back my head and curse the heavens,
Wallowing in my own disappointments,
Unaware you lie at my feet peering upward.
Your head cocked to the right, always to the right,
Asking … What are you doing?

From the throes of my infantile tantrum
I look down and see your confusion.
The anger leaves me so quickly I cannot breathe.
You cautiously rise to a hunched position,
And, ashamed, I glance away to the left, always to the left,
Wondering … What am I doing?

I babble my apologies for scaring you
And reach to embrace you, but you shy away,
Unsure of my intentions after all the ranting.
Human ways can be so confusing.
Now I truly understand the power of my anger,
Worrying … What do we do now?

I drop to all fours and lower my head,
Slowly, softly conjure up the best play growl I can muster,
Letting the sound roll roughly up my throat and out between my teeth.
You jump to your feet, leaping backward gracefully,
Into the game instantly, uncertainty forgotten,
As I gently bump your head with mine.

No more questions, no more hesitation.
You are my littermate, my pal.

Together
    Quiet close cuddles
    Raucous rib-bruising guffaws
    Rich companionship

Play
    Goofy circle runs
    Hopping dancing rings around
    Leap spin pirouette

P. P. Kadiddlehopper

P. P. Kadiddlehopper,
A gyrating show stopper,
Quite a lovely eye popper,
An energetic hip hopper,
A prolific poop plopper.
She's a cutesy bebopper,
With a tail like a limb lopper,
Which doubles as a floor mopper.
When eating she's a drool dropper.
She loves to be a bed flopper,
And sometimes pulls a real whopper.

Always, she's my wonderful, wagging, world-class chart topper.

Baton
    Mammoth munching mouth
    Clutching stick or mighty log
    Beware tender legs

Scraps
    Intense watchful gaze
    Food hitting floor mine mine mine
    Wait for permission

ready, set, go

up you git,
no longer sit,
we have a world to see.

out the door,
to search galore,
and welcome it with glee.

let's take a walk,
and have a talk,
explore from land to sea.

we'll have such fun,
play in the sun,
together, you and me.

Awaken
    Shadows snaking east
    Morning hush, canine rising
    Stretch full length wide yawn

Thrills
    Ride in countryside
    Eyes bright nose at the ready
    Horse cow ecstasy

Lilly's Song

Lilly Havannah, I really gotta hand it to ya, you are just as sweet as you can be. Lilly Lobelia, I'm glad that I could steal ya, And bring ya home to always live with me. Lilly Loquacious I have a yard that's spacious, Where you can run and play and just be free. Lilly Havannah, I really gotta hand it to ya, You are just as sweet as you can be. You're funny, you're smart, you tug at my heart, Lilly Havannah Angel lee

Troglodog

From the dark dawn of pre-history,
When your ancestors ran wild and vicious,
Bloody-jawed and killer-mad,
And slept burrowed in the earth,
Only a twitching nose, glowing eyes, and snarling lips
Visible to the approaching enemy.

Antediluvian
    Remember wild days
    Grazing on grass and berries
    Dine as ancestors

Smoglodog

To the smoggy daybreak of the 21st century
When your descendants cavort solicitously,
Soft-pawed and silly-minded,
Snuggling cozily beneath the blankets,
Only sonorous snores and the rising falling spread
A clue to the mysterious lump on the mattress.

Today
    Present to future
    Dog keeps pace with human race
    Constant companion

So Long For Now

We loved each other well
The days we were together.
I love you still
Though you are gone.

    I picture you a pup,
    Playing with abandon
    Among the rest
    Who went before.

        All the pain is gone.
        Your noble heart is healed.
        Great joy renewed.
        Bright soul refreshed.

            If there is truly balance
            Between the here and there,
            We'll reunite
            In love and play.

Aging
White muzzle gray face
Slower deliberate stride
Softly veiled wise eyes

Parting
Grief overwhelming
Life's sure flow abruptly changed
Soul bruised forever

Nancy L Reed: Love of the written word inspired Nancy to write from an early age—short stories, novels, memory snippets, readers theater scripts, poetry, and articles. She calls Colorado the perfect place to live and is Musing, at nancylreed.com, about building a tiny house designed specifically for a wordsmith. She finds fellow writers excellent company, and encourages everyone with a passion to tell a story to put pen to paper.

Janice Glenn,
Creator of Grr-ly

Sign up for the Wooden Pants Publishing newsletter at www.woodenpantspub.com for the latest news about authors and publications.

Made in the USA
San Bernardino, CA
21 October 2015